Walk in Love

Encounter the perfect love of Jesus

Learn how to truly love others

Pam Forster

Doorposts

This study is intended for use along with *The "Love Is" Chart*, available as a 16"x22" poster or an 8.5"x11" laminated chart.

ISBN 978-1-891206-63-4

Doorposts
5905 SW Lookingglass Drive,
Gaston, OR 97119
www.doorposts.com
888-433-4749

Contents

For Daddy,

whose love has made it a whole lot easier
for me to understand God's great love for me.

Many thanks – again – to Connie Meyerdierk,
for her editing, suggestions, and flexibility.

Introduction

"Therefore be imitators of God, as beloved children. And walk in love, as Christ loved us and gave himself up for us, a fragrant offering and sacrifice to God" (Eph. 5:2).

If you're holding this book in your hands, it's probably because you see **the need for more love** in your home. We're all sinners and loving others doesn't come naturally to any of us.

1 Corinthians 13 is a great place to head for a better understanding of love. Paul's description of love shows up at weddings and in frames on the walls of our homes. We find its short phrases in the lyrics of songs and in illustrated board books for little ones. In 1 Corinthians 13 we find a concise but beautiful summary of godly love.

It's beautiful, but it's written to a group of people who *were not loving each other very well.* They were squabbling and arguing about whose God-given gifts in the church were the most important. They were trying to one-up each other and envying those who looked more important or successful than they were. When Paul wrote this letter to the members of the Corinthian church, he was addressing their *lack of love* and showing them what real love looks like.

1 Corinthians 13 is written for non-lovers. It's for people who need to *meet* love, not just try to *do* love.

Love is a Person.

Have you ever noticed that the passage isn't presented as a list of *commands*? Paul doesn't start out by saying, "Suffer long. Be kind. Don't envy. Don't brag. Don't be arrogant..." Instead of telling us what to do, he tells us what *love* does. He *personifies* love. He speaks of it as a person.

That's because love *is* a person.

> *"Anyone who does not love does not know God, because **God is love**"* (1 John 4:8).

Try this. Read 1 Corinthians 13:4-7 and replace the word *love* (or *charity,* if you're reading the King James Version) with the word *God.*

> *God* is patient and kind. *God* does not envy or boast. *God* is not arrogant or rude.

Then do the same thing, this time inserting the word *Jesus* in the place of love. Jesus was God's love in human form, living among us.

> *Jesus* is patient and kind. *Jesus* does not envy or boast. *Jesus* is not arrogant or rude.

Love *is* a person. **It's God.**

God's love will change you.

Before we can love with a godly love, we need to *meet* love. We need to *experience* love. We need to understand *how deeply we are loved.*

When we really start to understand how much God loves us, the God-shaped hollow spot inside of us will finally be filled up. We won't be expecting *people* to meet a need in our soul that only God can meet. We'll be able reach out to meet *their* needs instead of looking to them to meet *our* needs.

We will be able to love without needing to be loved in return, and that's when love really becomes *love* – godly, self-sacrificial, for-the-good-of-others love – the kind of love described in 1 Corinthians 13.

That's what we want to see as we take a closer look at 1 Corinthians 13. Let's take the time to *meet* love and to understand how much we *are* loved. Let's slow down and look at how God loves us, and how He loved us through His Son.

How to guide your family through this study

As you go through this book, take your time. Each short chapter is divided into several sections. *Resist the urge to skip over sections.* You may decide you only want to look at two or three verses at a time, if you have small children.

- Read and discuss the **short descriptions of love** at the beginning of each section.
- Then use several short study times, if necessary, to look up *each* of the **verses about God's love**. *Read from a translation your children can understand.* Talk about each verse or passage. Pull up an online commentary for help if you run into verses you find hard to explain. (www.Blueletterbible.org or www.Biblestudytools.com are both great sites, if you need help.)

  (**If your children can read**, this is a great opportunity to let them practice looking up verses in the Bible. You can make the process even more exciting by using these verses for Bible drills. Have all the children close their Bibles, state the Bible reference for them, then shout "Go!" and let them see who can find the verse first. When everyone has found the verse, let the "winner" read it aloud.)
- Then do the same with the **verses about Jesus's love**. Really take the time to *see* how much God loves us, and to learn from Jesus's perfect example of love.
- Then **read the other verses** that tell us more about the particular aspect of love being studied in the chapter.
- Choose *at least one* verse from each chapter to **memorize** together, and complete *at least one* of the **practical projects** at the end of each chapter.
- As you finish up each chapter, **end with a time of prayer**, thanking God for His great love for you and asking Him to help you share that love with others.

As you study and apply what you are learning together, **don't let these verses** (and especially the chart, if you're using it) **become a to-do list.** Think of it more as a **poem of praise** for love – love made flesh in the person of Jesus. Soak your children in the bath of God's love. Help them understand that God loves them so much that He gave His only Son to die a horrible death in their place.

Help them appreciate how Christ's perfect life and undeserved death paid the debt for their sins and restored their relationship with God. They don't have to earn God's love and approval. *They already have it.* If they've placed their faith in Jesus, God looks at them and sees His perfect Son. They're forgiven. They're loved.

When they really believe and rest in God's love, they will be ready – and empowered – to love others with the same kind of love.

"…just as I have loved you, you also are to love one another" (John 13:34).

Love is Patient.

Are you being patient – or are you upset?

"Above all, keep loving one another earnestly, since love covers a multitude of sins" (1 Peter 4:8).

We live in an imperfect world with imperfect people. Sometimes we will be wronged by others, so we need to learn how to respond in a godly way when someone sins against us or does something we don't like. Being patient toward those who bother us pleases God, while getting angry at others will hurt our relationships, make us unhappy, and dishonor God.

Patience is "long-tempered".

The Greek word in this verse is made up of two words – *long* and *temper*. It's telling us love is *long-tempered*. A short-tempered person gets angry quickly; a long-tempered person remains calm.

- Love remembers how patient God is with us, and tries to patiently love others in the same way.
- Love doesn't speak or behave in an unkind, angry, or violent manner.
- Love puts up with many slights, hurts, and wrongs without getting angry.
- Love doesn't try to get even.
- A loving person doesn't stop loving someone who has hurt him. He continues to show him love, just as God chooses to love us, even when we sin.
- Love keeps calm, choosing to trust God to know what is best and to take care of the situation.
- Love goes to a person who is seriously sinning against him and discusses the problem with a humble and loving attitude. If he won't listen, he brings in others who want to help the wrongdoer be delivered from his sin.
- Love patiently gives a person time to become the person God has designed him to be.

God is patient with us.

Ps. 86:15. How is God described?

Neh. 9:17. How did the Israelites respond to the miracles God performed for them when they left Egypt? What was God's response? How is God described?

2 Pet. 3:9. Why is God patient with us?

Rom. 2:3-4. Why is God kind and patient with us?

Ps. 103:10. Has God treated us the way we deserve to be treated?

Isa. 48:9. Why does God say He holds back His anger?

Neh. 9:30-31. What did God do after warning His people for forty years? Does He just overlook sin and never discipline us for it? What is true of God even when He is disciplining His children?

Reread the verses listed above and note the other attributes of God that are listed along with patience or longsuffering in each verse. Are these qualities that we should also seek to imitate?

Additional verses to read and discuss: Acts 13:18; Isa. 53:3; Ps. 78:38; Ps. 103:8; Ps. 145:8; Joel 2:13; Jonah 4:2; James 5:10

If God is patient with us, who have sinned against Him over and over, how should we respond to the much smaller slights and sins of others toward us?

Jesus's love is patient.

Isa. 53:3. How did man treat Jesus? What did He do for man in return?

Luke 22:47-51. How did Jesus respond to Judas's betrayal of Him? What could He have done if He had chosen to? What did Jesus say and do when Peter cut off the soldier's ear? What can we learn from His example?

1 Pet. 2:21-25. What kind of example did Jesus leave for us? Was He guilty of sin? How did He respond to the scornful speech of others? What did He not do when He was suffering? What did He do instead? Why did He die on the cross?

What did His suffering accomplish for us? What can we learn from His example?

Heb. 4:15-16. Why is Jesus compassionate toward us in our weakness? How did He respond to temptation? Because of this, what can we do with confidence? How should we treat people who are weak and imperfect like us?

Additional passages to read and discuss. Note each of the weaknesses and wrongs Jesus was willing to patiently bear. Mark. 1:35-38; Matt. 9:2-7; Matt. 12:24; Matt. 26:36-75; Matt. 27:13-14; John 8:59

Jesus was patient and willing to suffer wrongs for our sake because of His great love for us. Because He loves us, shouldn't we be willing to suffer the much smaller wrongs that others commit against us?

The Bible teaches us about patience.

Eccles. 7:8. What two kinds of attitudes are being compared? What do we usually think of as the opposite of pride? Why would being humble – thinking less about our selves – make it easier to be patient with others? How could someone who is patient be better than someone who is proud?

Prov. 16:32. How could a patient person be better than a mighty soldier who conquers a city? What does it mean to rule our spirit?

Prov. 14:29. What might the patient person understand about other people and their weaknesses? How would this help him remain patient when slighted or wronged? What might he understand about God that helps him control his anger? What does the quick-tempered person reveal about himself? What is he allowing to rule him?

James 1:19-20. What should we be quick to do? What should we be slow to do? How could being quick to listen help us be slow to anger?

Rom. 8:28. How will this truth help us be patient with difficult people and circumstances?

Gal. 5:14. How will loving others like we love ourselves help us be patient with them?

Col. 3:12. When we take off impatience and anger, what should we put on in their place?

Additional passages to read and discuss: Eccles. 7:9; Prov. 20:3; Eph. 4:1-2; Rom. 12:18-19

Love patiently.

- **Act out these situations** with the family. How would you show longsuffering in each case?
  - Your brother breaks a vase in the living room, then blames you for doing it.
  - Someone makes fun of the clothes you are wearing.
  - Your brother cries and takes away the toy you are playing with.
  - Your sister doesn't clean up her side of the bedroom.
  - A friend who is visiting your home doesn't want to play anything you want to play.
  - Someone is pointing and whispering about you across the room.
- **Stop and pray** before you speak or react to someone who has wronged you. Pray for God's blessing on this person, and ask for His help to be a picture of His love and patience.
- **Ask yourself** if this issue is really worth the energy you're investing in it. Are you making yourself and your feelings more important than loving others the way Jesus loves you?
- **Choose to "take off"** complaining, anger, and the desire for revenge, and to put on longsuffering and patience.
- Channel your frustration and anger into **attacking the problem**, not the person. What can you do to make the situation better? What can you change? What do you need to patiently endure, trusting God to know what is best?
- When you are tempted to be impatient and angry, **recite one of the verses** you have memorized, and pray for God's help. Jesus has been tempted in the same way.
- **Remember** how much God loves you. Think of Jesus suffering in order to save you. Can you be patient with these small injuries from others, when He suffered so much more for you?

Give thanks.

- Thank God for sending Jesus to die for you, and for giving you the free gift of salvation, even though you've done nothing to deserve it. If you haven't yet put your faith in Christ's saving work on the cross, thank God for His patience and for drawing you to Him, and repent.
- Thank Him for His patient love as He helps you to become more like His Son.
- Thank Jesus for being born as a man, and for living a life without sin in the midst of people who hurt Him and sinned against Him.
- Thank Him for the strength His love gives you to love others, no matter how they treat you.

Love is Kind.

Are you being helpful – or uncaring?

"If I then, your Lord and Teacher, have washed your feet, you also ought to wash one another's feet" (John 13:14).

The kindness God has shown to us is the same kindness He wants us to show to others. He doesn't love us just to love us. He loves us so He can show His love to others through us as we learn how to love like He loves. The more we know Jesus, the better we'll be able to show His kindness to others.

Kindness means caring about others and helping them.

The Greek word for *kindness* in 1 Corinthians 13:4 is only used this one time in the entire New Testament. It means *to show oneself mild, to be kind, to use kindness.* It is an active word. Kindness isn't just how we feel. It's what we *do.*

- Love treats others the way it would want to be treated.
- Love *searches* for opportunities to do good to all.
- Love sees a need and *does something about it.*
- A loving person seeks to add to the comfort and happiness of others with his words, his actions, and his belongings.
- Love cheerfully gives to others, without expecting anything in return.
- A loving person shows kindness to undeserving people because he realizes that *he* doesn't deserve the love and kindness that God has shown to *him.*
- Love helps people who are suffering and does what it can to make their burdens lighter, remembering that Jesus helps carry our burdens.
- A loving person gives up what is his in order to help others, remembering that Jesus gave up His *life* to save *us.*
- A loving person is generous, knowing that God will continue to take care of him.
- Love serves Jesus by serving others.
- Love helps others in a way that builds them up and respects them as people made in God's image.

God is kind to us.

Titus 2:11. What has God graciously given to us?

John 3:16. Who and what did God give to the world because of His love?

Rom. 5:8. How did God show His love to us while we were still sinners?

Titus 3:4-5. What appeared when God saved us? Does our salvation have anything to do with our own works? According to what did God save us? Should we only show kindness to those who deserve it?

Eph. 2:4-5. What is God rich in? Why did God save us? What was our condition when God chose to make us alive in Christ? Did we do anything to deserve new life?

Eph. 2:6-7. Why has God raised us up with Jesus and seated us in the heavenly places?

Eph. 2:8-9. How have we been saved? Do we do anything to earn salvation? Who is the gift of salvation from?

Matt. 5:44-45. On whom does God make the sun rise? On whom does He send rain? So how should we treat our enemies?

God is kind to us when we deserve nothing more than judgment for our sins. Shouldn't we want to show that same kindness to others?

Jesus's love is kind.

Isa. 53:4. What has Jesus carried for us?

Rom. 5:6. What was our condition when Jesus died for us? For whom did He die?

Eph. 1:7. Whose blood earned our salvation? What are we forgiven because of the riches of God's grace?

Matt. 9:35. What kinds of things did Jesus do?

Matt. 9:36. What did Jesus feel for the crowds? Why? What should we feel for those who are without Jesus?

Matt. 15:32-39. What was Jesus concerned about for the crowd? What did He do about it?

John 13:2-5. What did Jesus know about Judas when He washed the disciples' feet? Do you think He still washed Judas's feet?

John 13:12-15. What did Jesus tell the disciples they should do, since He, their Master, had washed their feet? Why did He give us His example?

Matt. 9:10-13. Why did Jesus say He ate with tax collectors and sinners?

Read about Jesus's miracles. What kinds of needs did Jesus meet when He performed miracles? Mark 1:32-34; Mark 1:40-42; Mark 2:1-5; Luke 7:11-17; Matt. 8:1-3; Matt. 9:18-26; Mark 5:21-43; Luke 8:40-56; Luke 13:10-13; John 2:1-12; Matt. 8:14-17

Was Jesus too busy, too poor, too indifferent, too important, or too proud to be kind to others? He showed great kindness and compassion for others, and He's shown great kindness to us. Because He loves us, we are able to show His love to others through our acts of kindness.

The Bible teaches us about kindness.

Acts 20:35. Which is better, giving or receiving? Which do you do most? In what ways can you be a giver today?

1 John 3:17. Can God's love be in our hearts, if we are able to help meet a brother's need but choose not to do so?

Luke 6:31. How should we treat others?

Luke 6:38. How much will be given back to us when we give?

Heb. 13:16. Why should we do good and share?

Eph. 2:10. Who made us new in Christ? Why? What has God prepared for us?

Gal. 6:10. To whom should we do good? How often should we do good?

1 John 3:18. How are we supposed to love others? Are words enough?

James 2:15-16. Are we helping others who have physical needs if we only talk to them but don't give them what they need?

2 Thess. 3:13. What should we not get tired of doing?

Ps. 141:5. Why would it be a kindness for a godly man to correct us when he sees us sinning?

Additional passages to read and discuss: Ps. 18:25a; Prov. 11:17, Prov. 11:25; Prov. 19:17; Col. 3:12; Matt. 25:34-40; Prov. 14:21; Luke 10:30-37; Rom. 12:13; 1 Pet. 4:9; Matt. 5:43-48; 2 Cor. 9:6-7

Love with kind actions.

- **Pray** every morning for God to help you see the many opportunities you have to be kind to others. As you go through the day, focus on treating others the way you would want to be treated. Before you go to someone's house, into a store, to church, to the doctor, etc., ask God to help you see ways you can show kindness to the people who are there.
- Who do you know who has been **unkind to you**? Go out of your way to be kind to that person.
- Are you kind to the people in **your own family**? Think of specific ways you can show kindness to your parents and each of your siblings. Who needs help? Who needs encouragement? Who needs some extra loving? Do everything you can to be kind to them every day!
- **Find a way to earn money.** Before you spend any of your earnings on yourself, put part of it in the offering at church, and use another part of it to help or encourage someone else.
- **Read Luke 14:12-14.** Then plan a little party, meal, or other special occasion for people who will not be able to return your hospitality. Think of neighbors, children in a hospital or orphanage, the elderly at home or in care centers, etc.

Give thanks.

- Thank God for the faithful, generous way He takes care of you and provides for you, and for the privilege of sharing what He has given you with others.
- Thank God for all the kind people He has put in your life and the difference they have made in your life.
- Thank Him for His kindness in giving us the gift of salvation, when we can do nothing to earn or deserve it.
- Thank God for His love that continues to give, no matter what, and ask Him for the grace to show that sort of kindness to others.
- Thank Jesus for reaching out and doing good for you.

Love does not envy.

Are you happy for others – or do you envy them?

"...though he was rich, yet for your sake he became poor, so that you by his poverty might become rich" (2 Corinthians 8:9b).

We can't love someone and envy him at the same time. Envy resents the good that others have and experience. Love wants the best for them.

Love is happy for others. Envy is never satisfied.

The Greek word in this verse means, *to burn with zeal* or *to be heated or to boil with envy, hatred, anger*. Zeal can be a good thing. When Jesus cleared the moneychangers out of the temple, He was rightly angry for the wrongs that were being committed in His place of worship.

When our zeal is focused on ourselves, it becomes envy. When a person envies someone, he is not loving him. Instead, he dislikes and may even hate a person who has more than he does or is better than he is. If we're eager to do good to all, we can't wish ill on any. Love rejoices in the blessings and prosperity of others.

- Love is happy when others are doing well. Envy is resentful.
- Love wants the best for others. Envy wants to hurt those who are more blessed or happy than it.
- A loving person is happy in the position God has placed him, because he believes He knows what is best for him. An envious person is always looking for more.
- Love enjoys what it has because it understands that it doesn't deserve anything from God except judgment for sin. Envy is miserable because it thinks it deserves more than it's been given.
- Love is sorry when someone gets in trouble. Envy is glad because it makes himself look better.
- A loving person remembers that talents and riches are blessings God gives as He chooses, so he doesn't get upset when others receive different blessings. An envious person doesn't want anyone to do better or have more than he does.
- Love admires people who excel. Envy resents and dislikes them, and tries to minimize their abilities.
- Love's happiness is based on its relationship with God. Envy tries to be happy by outdoing others.
- Love is willing to share its friends with others. Envy tries to keep them all to itself.
- A loving person doesn't worry about prosperous sinners because he remembers that they will someday be judged. An envious person is tempted to be angry with God when it sees sinners doing better than he is.

God is not envious. He wants good for us.

2 Tim. 1:9. Who saved us? Who has set us apart for Himself? Why did He do this? When did He do this? Does He want what is best for us or is He worried about giving us more than we deserve?

Rom. 5:8. How did God demonstrate His love for us? Did He wait until we were perfect, or until *we* loved Him?

Eph. 1:5-6. Did God just save us from hell? What did God make us when He adopted us? Who is our brother now? Does God begrudge us the great honor of being called His sons? Did Jesus object?

Gal. 4:4-7. What did God do so that we could be adopted as His sons? What else are we when we are sons? With whom do we share that privilege?

God hasn't held back anything in order to save us. He gave His only Son, He adopted us as His children, He made us heirs together with Christ. He is wants to bless us richly. Should we envy His blessings in other people's lives? Or should we rejoice with them?

Jesus's love is not envious.

2 Cor. 8:9b. What did Jesus become so that we could become rich? Did He think that was unfair?

Phil. 2: 5-7. Did Jesus try to hang on to His equality with God? What did He do instead?

John 5:30. Did Jesus begrudge the Father's authority over Him?

John 4:34. Was Jesus content in the position the Father had placed Him in?

Rev. 1:5-6. Did Jesus just love us? Did He just do what He had to do to save us from our sins? What else did He do? Was He worried about blessing us too much?

John 17:22. Did Jesus want to keep the glory the Father gave Him all to Himself? What did He do with it? Why?

John 14:12. Was Jesus worried about others doing greater works than He did?

Matt. 8:20. What did Jesus not have?

Jesus went without many things as a man. He was born in a stable. His earthly father was a simple carpenter. He didn't even have a home during His years of ministry. He willingly gave up the glory of heaven and lived a humble life, giving up everything for us. Shouldn't we be content in Him and rejoice with those He chooses to bless in different ways than He has us?

The Bible teaches us about envy.

1 Cor. 3:3. Why should we not behave like "mere men"?

2 Cor. 12:20. What other sins are associated with envy? Is it peaceful when these sins are present? Do you see love mentioned along with envy in this verse?

Rom. 12:15. What should we do with others who are happy? What should we do with those who are sad?

Phil. 2:3. What is rivalry? What should we do instead of trying to be better than others? Did Jesus compete with others?

Phil. 4:11. What had Paul learned? Was Jesus content with His circumstances?

Prov. 14:30. What does envy do to us? How does a peaceful heart affect us?

Ps. 49:16-17. Why should we not worry when unbelievers prosper?

James 3:16. What else will be present when jealousy and selfish ambition exist?

Matt. 6:33. What should we want most?

Matt. 6:19-21. Where should we *not* lay up treasure? Where should we? Why?

Additional passages to read and discuss: Gal. 5:21; 1 Pet. 2:1, Ps. 73:3, 16-18; Prov. 27:4; Titus 3:3-7

Love joyfully.

- **Discuss the different ways you might envy someone** (being a bad sport in a game: trying to take a toy away from someone when they start playing with it: being angry or unhappy when someone wins a prize, gets a special present, goes on an exciting vacation, does better on a school assignment, etc., wanting to be as popular as someone else, being uncooperative when someone has been put in charge of you, etc.) Review what you have learned in this lesson and how it applies to these situations. Are you loving people when you envy them? Why not?
- **Read and dramatize the following accounts of people in the Bible who were envious.** Then act it out again, this time without envy. For example, what would the prodigal son's brother do if he wasn't mad about his brother getting a party he didn't think he deserved? Cain (Gen. 4:3-8 and 1 John 3:12), Jews with Jesus (Matt. 27:11-25), brother of prodigal son (Luke 15:25-32), Joseph's brothers (Gen. 37:4-20 and Acts 7:9), Haman (Est. 6:6-12), Saul (1 Sam. 18:7-9).
- **Read and act out the parable of the vineyard workers in Matt. 20:1-16.** How does this parable relate to the sin of envy? What can you learn from it? Act out the story again, and have the workers be happy with what the boss paid them.
- **Learn to congratulate people who have done well.** What should you say? What should you do?
- **Read one of the Gospels** and notice each time Jesus is envied by others and each time He chooses to not envy others. What did He do without? What did He subject Himself to, even though He was God?
- If you find yourself in a situation where **confusion and strife** are present, stop and ask, "Am I being envious?" If you are, confess it and repent.

Give thanks.

- Thank God for choosing not only to save you, but to make you His child and an heir together with Christ.
- Thank God for His many blessings in your life, none of which you deserve.
- Thank Him for loving you and giving you what He knows is best for you.
- Thank Him for blessing others, too, in the way He knows is best.
- Thank Jesus for willingly living a life of hardship and poverty for your sake.

Love does not boast.

Are you being modest – or are you looking for glory?

"Have this mind among yourselves, which is yours in Christ Jesus, who, though he was in the form of God, did not count equality with God a thing to be grasped, but emptied himself, by taking the form of a servant, being born in the likeness of men" (Philippians 2:5-7).

Love keeps us from envying what *others* have. Love also keeps us from bragging about what *we* have.

It's impossible to love and boast at the same time. The braggart wants everyone's attention on himself, but love focuses attention on others.

Love is modest. Boasting seeks to bring glory to itself.

The Greek word for *boasting* in 1 Corinthians 13:4 speaks of *self display*. When we boast, we are putting ourselves - or what we want other people to think about us - on display for others.

If we are truly loving others, we won't be putting ourselves on display, because we value the people we love more than we value ourselves. We can't love and be conceited and proud at the same time.

- Love remembers that we are totally dependent on God, and that everything we are, and everything we have, is a gift from Him. Boasting tries to take the credit for itself.
- Love remembers how great God is and how He in His grace has chosen to bless us, even though we don't deserve it. Boasting takes the credit for itself.
- Love focuses on others. Boasting is absorbed with self.
- Love doesn't focus on talking about itself. Boasting promotes itself.
- Love listens more than it talks. Boasting talks more than it listens.
- Love is honest and humble. Boasting wants to impress.
- Love doesn't insist on being the center of attention. Boasting seeks the spotlight.
- Love is quiet about its kindnesses and good deeds. Boasting wants people to know what it has done.
- Love realizes it needs Jesus. Boasting tries to prove its own worth.
- Love is secure in God's undeserved love. Boasting is insecure and wants to know that it matters and is loved.
- Love has integrity. Boasting uses things like clothes, friends, social events, and possessions to boost its image.
- Love admits when it is wrong. Boasting makes excuses and blames others.

- Love is careful to not offend when speaking of its accomplishments and blessings in the presence of those less gifted or blessed. Boasting uses those people to bolster its own opinion of itself.
- Love gives due honor and credit to others. Boasting claims all honor and credit for itself.
- Love gives glory to God. Boasting robs God by forgetting that everything comes from Him, and that all the credit goes to Him.
- Love will be rewarded for its good deeds. Boasting gives up any reward for the good it has done.

God doesn't boast about His glory.

God doesn't boast. He doesn't need to because *nobody* is greater than He is.

Read the following verses and note who or what is praising God: Ps. 19:1; Ps. 22:23; Ps. 69:34; Ps. 89:5; Ps. 98:4; Ps. 145:1-3, 10; Ps. 148:1-14; Ps. 150:6

God has done great things. He doesn't need to boast about Himself. If God, in all His glory, doesn't boast, do we really have anything to boast about? All creation will praise Him. Shouldn't *we* be busy praising *Him* instead of praising ourselves?

Jesus's love is modest.

2 Cor. 5:21. What did Jesus become for us? Why?

Phil. 2:7. What did Jesus make Himself?

John 5:30. What did Jesus say He could do in His own strength? Whose will was He seeking?

John 7:3-6. What did Jesus's brothers want Him to do? Why? How did Jesus respond?

Luke 4:22. What did the people ask about Jesus? Did He take the opportunity to point out that He was *God's* Son?

John 8:48-50. Who does Jesus say He is honoring? Who are the Jews dishonoring? What does Jesus say about His own glory?

John 14:13. Who was Jesus concerned about glorifying?

Matt. 3:13-15. How did John the Baptist feel about baptizing Jesus? What was Jesus's response?

Mark 6:2. What did the people say when they heard Jesus preaching in the synagogue?

John 18:33-37. How did Jesus respond to Pilate's questions? How *could* He have truthfully responded?

Jesus knew His Father loved Him, so it didn't matter what others thought of Him. He didn't need to boast about who He was or what He could do. He could continue loving the people God had given Him to love, whether they accepted Him and acknowledged Him as God's Son or not.

If we know God loves us, should it matter what others think of us? Do we need to boast to win people's favor, or should we focus on loving them, like He loves us?

The Bible teaches us about boasting.

Isa. 10:15. Does an axe have the right to brag about what it's cutting? Is the saw better than the man using it? Do we have the right to brag about what we are or do when God is the one who makes it all possible?

Jer. 9:23-24. Are we supposed to boast about our wisdom, strength, or riches? So should we boast about how well we do in school, how athletic we are, or how much stuff we have? What should we boast in instead?

Luke 17:10. What should our attitude be when we have obeyed God? Should we brag about it?

Ps. 115:1. Who should receive glory instead of us? Why?

Prov. 27:2. Who should praise us? Who shouldn't praise us?

Prov. 25:27. What happens when we eat too much honey? What happens when we seek our own glory?

1 Cor. 4: 7. Do you have anything that you didn't receive? So do you have any right to boast about it?

Matt. 23:12. What happens when we exalt ourselves? What happens when we humble ourselves?

Additional passages to read and discuss: Ps. 34:2-3; Gal. 6:14; Prov. 30:32; 1 Cor. 16:9

Love modestly.

- Show **kindness to someone secretly**. Don't tell anyone what you did.
- **Thank your parents and grandparents** for loving you and taking care of you, teaching you, encouraging you, and giving you the things you have.
- Practice responding to a **compliment politely**.
- Learn how to ask **polite questions** to help you get to know other people better instead of just talking about yourself.
- Pray and ask God to help you see **the many ways you are proud**. Repent of your pride and thank God for His love and patience with you.

Give thanks.

- Thank God for making you, taking care of you, and giving you the family, talents, and opportunities He has given you.
- Thank God for loving you without you having to do anything to deserve His love.
- Thank Him for creating you with a purpose, and for equipping you to fulfill that purpose.
- Thank Jesus for giving up the glory of heaven to become a man, so that you could share His glory with Him for eternity.
- Thank Jesus for taking on the punishment of sin for you, even though He lived a sinless life, so that you could be saved from sin.
- Thank Him for choosing to lose His glory and His Father's love and approval while He was taking the punishment for all our sins, so that He could win the Father's approval and forgiveness for you.

Love is not arrogant.

Are you being humble – or do you think you're better than others?

"But I am among you as the one who serves" (Luke 22:27b).

An arrogant person has an inflated view of his own ideas and abilities. He is like a balloon filled with air, puffed up with pride in himself, and looking down on others. When we think so highly of ourselves, we don't know how to love others.

Love is humble. Arrogance thinks it's better than others.

The Greek word for *arrogant* or *puffed up* in 1 Corinthians 13:4 means *to inflate, to blow up, to cause to swell up*. Humility isn't puffed up. It's doesn't think about itself, because it's busy thinking about Jesus and about others. A humble person is more interested in others than he is about himself. He knows he is totally dependent on God, and recognizes that he is a helpless sinner who needs God's forgiveness – just like everyone else does.

- Love remembers that we're lost without Jesus. Arrogance thinks it's just fine on its own.
- A loving person doesn't think about himself. An arrogant person wants everyone to think about and honor him.
- Love serves others. Arrogance expects to be served.
- Love looks for ways to be useful to others. Arrogance looks for ways to use others.
- Love doesn't think it's better or more important than others. Arrogance looks down on others.
- Love realizes it could be wrong. Arrogance thinks it is right.
- Love thinks of others. Arrogance is too full of itself to think about the needs and comforts of others.
- Love is quiet about its accomplishments and possessions. Arrogance is a show-off.
- Love thinks others have good ideas. Arrogance expects others to do what it wants and agree with what it thinks.
- Love is thankful for God's gifts. Arrogance thinks it has earned them.
- Love waits to be invited. Arrogance takes the biggest and the best.

God's love is humble. He stoops down from heaven to love and save us.

Deut. 7:7. Did Jesus choose His people Israel because of anything special about them? Why *did* He choose them?

Ps. 138:6. How does God treat the lowly, even though He is high? How does He treat the arrogant?

Ps. 113:4-7. Where is God? How does he treat the poor and the needy?

Isa. 57:15. Where does God dwell? Who does God dwell with? Why?

Ps. 144:3. Who does God regard and think of, even though He is God?

Ps. 103:4. What does God redeem us from? What does He crown us with?

Rom. 5:8. What did our holy God do while we were still sinners?

1 John 4:10. What did God do because He loved us?

The God who created us and everything else that exists stooped down from heaven and saved us. If we put our faith in Jesus, God forgives. We can quit pretending that we're good enough for God by trying to look better than other people. God accepts us just as we are because our sins are all paid for by Jesus. Because God has accepted us, shouldn't we have the grace to love and accept others, just as they are?

Jesus's love is humble.

Luke 22:27b. What role did Jesus assume while living among men on earth?

Mark 10:43-45. If we desire to be great, what must we be? If we desire to be first, what must we be? Who is our example? What did Jesus come to do?

John 7:1- 9. What did Jesus's brothers want Him to do? Why? Did Jesus take their advice?

Luke 5:27. Did Jesus look down on tax collectors like most people of His day?

Luke 7:34. Of what did the Pharisees accuse Jesus. Why?

Isa. 53:2-3. What was Jesus, God's Son, like when He lived on earth? How did people treat Him? Did He have to do this?

Matt. 20:28. What did Jesus *not* come to do? What *did* He come to do?

Matt. 11:29. How does Jesus describe Himself?

John 6:38. Where did Jesus come down from? Why did He come?

Heb. 2:11. What is Jesus not ashamed to call us?

Luke 2:7. Where was Jesus born? Why? Is this a fitting birthplace for a king?

Luke 2:51. Did Jesus think He was too important to obey His parents?

Matt. 19:13-15. Did Jesus think He was too important to spend time with children?

John 4:5-9. Why was the Samaritan woman surprised when Jesus spoke to her?

John 13:4-5. What did Jesus do for the disciples? Was this a normal job for a master?

1 Pet. 2:24. What kind of shameful death was Jesus willing to die so that we could be healed?

Isa. 50:6. Did Jesus think He was too important to be treated the way He was?

Additional passages to read and discuss: John 1:14; Rom. 8:3; Heb. 2:9; Matt. 21:5-9; John 5:19; Matt. 9:9-13; 2 Cor. 8:9; Gal. 3:13; John 8:48-50; John 1:11; Phil. 2:6-7

Jesus gave up the glories of heaven and humbled Himself by becoming a man and dying on the cross for us. If He loves us that much, do we need to worry about whether others are impressed with us? If we love Him in return and long to please Him, will our eyes be on ourselves all the time, or will they be on Him and on the people He wants us to love?

The Bible teaches us about arrogance.

Rom. 12:16. What is harmony? What should we do instead of being haughty? What should we never be?

Prov. 16:5. How does God feel about the arrogant person? What will happen to him?

Prov. 26:12. How much hope is there for someone who is wise in his own eyes?

Phil. 2:3. What should we do instead of trying to be better than other people?

Rom. 7:18. Does anything good dwell in us without Jesus? So do we have anything to be proud of in ourselves?

Prov. 13:10. What is the only thing that comes from insolence or arrogance? What do those who take advice have?

Isa. 2:11. What will happen to haughty looks? What will happen to man's pride? Who is the only one who will be truly exalted?

Prov. 18:12. What is a man's heart like before destruction? What is it like before he is honored?

Prov. 8:13. What should we hate if we fear the Lord?

Ps. 101:5. What does God think about the haughty, arrogant person?

Jer. 45:5a. Should we seek great things for ourselves? In what ways do you seek great things for yourself?

Ps. 131:1-2. What should we do instead of being arrogant?

Matt. 20:26-27. What must we be to be great?

Additional passages to read and discuss: Gal. 5:24-26; Rom. 12:3; Prov. 25:6-7; John 13:12-17

Love humbly.

- We become humble when we take our focus off of ourselves and start falling in love with Jesus. **Read the Gospels** – Matthew, then Mark and Luke and John – with your family. Remember while you are reading that Jesus was a real person who chose to live a real life among us, even though He was God. Watch how He treats other people. Read about the suffering He endured to save you from sin and make you his brother or sister.
- **Read Luke 18:11-14.** Then act out the story. Who was humble? Who understood how small and sinful he was compared to God? Who did Jesus say would be exalted?
- **Find a balloon and a small box.** Blow up the balloon and put it inside the box. How much room is left in the box for anything else? When we're inflated with our opinion of ourselves, there's not much room left in our hearts or our lives for thinking about others.

Give thanks.

- Thank God for caring about *you* while He oversees all that He created and sustains.
- Thank God for loving you, saving you and making you His child.
- Thank Him for the blessings, privileges, and abilities He has given you, and ask Him to help you use them to serve and please Him.
- Thank Jesus for humbling Himself and becoming a man who suffered and died for *you* so that you could become God's child.

Love is not rude.

Are you being courteous – or rude?

"And Jesus increased in wisdom and in stature and in favor with God and man" (Luke 2:52).

We can't love someone and be rude to him. If we love him we think about what is good and pleasant for him. When we're rude, we're just thinking about ourselves and what pleases us.

Love is courteous.

The Greek word for **rude** in 1 Corinthians 13:5 comes from a word that means "deformed". One dictionary defines *deformed* as, *"not having the normal or expected shape, especially because of a problem in the way something has developed or grown".* When we're rude we have a problem in the way we're growing. We're not growing in our ability to love others and treat them with honor and respect. We're not conformed to Christ's image.

- Love considers others more important than itself and demonstrates that with its actions. Rudeness thinks about its own convenience.
- Love thinks about the comforts and needs of others. Rudeness considers its own comfort.
- Love honors and respects others. Rudeness is disrespectful.
- Love practices good manners as a way of honoring others. Rudeness acts as if others are not there.
- Love puts others at ease. Rudeness makes them uncomfortable.
- Love controls itself for the sake of others. Rudeness does what it feels like doing whether others like it or not.
- Love dresses, speaks, and behaves in ways that are appropriate to the occasion and place. Rudeness does what it wants to do.
- Love is pleasant to be around. Rudeness shames and embarrasses.
- Love stops to think about what it is going to say before it speaks. Rudeness speaks before it thinks.

God is courteous to us.

Gen. 3:1-21. How did God speak to Adam and Eve, even though He knew they had disobeyed Him? How did He respond when Eve blamed the serpent and Adam blamed Eve? Even though He had to discipline them, what did He make for them? (Even while Adam and Eve were disobeying, God already had a plan for saving them.)

Ex. 33:11. How did God speak to Moses, even though He is God?

Jer. 29:11. What kind of thoughts does God have toward us?

Jer. 31:3. How has God drawn us to Himself?

Ps. 18:35. What makes us great?

Eph. 2:4-6. Did God leave us dead in our sins? Where, instead, has He called us to sit?

God has shown great courtesy and kindness to us. He stooped down from heaven and made a way for us to become His children, even though we were in rebellion against Him. He has called us to sit with Jesus and to reign with Him. If God has shown so much favor to us, shouldn't we go out of our way to be courteous and thoughtful to others, no matter who they are?

Jesus's love is courteous.

1 John 3:5. Why did Jesus become a man? Did he sin? How does this mean He treated other people?

Luke 2:52. What four things are said about Jesus? How do you think He treated others, if these four things are true? Can they be said about you?

2 Cor. 10:1. How does Paul describe Jesus?

Luke 7:36-50. Did Jesus turn down the Pharisee's invitation to eat with him? How did Jesus treat the woman who came to Him? How did Jesus respond to the Pharisee's remarks? Was He grateful for the woman's kindness to Him? Did He argue with those who didn't like what He was doing and saying?

Mark 10:13-16. How did Jesus respond when the disciples turned away people who brought their children for Him to touch? What did He do with the children?

Matt. 27:11. How did Jesus respond to Pilate's questions? What was Pilate's response?

John 19:26. Who was Jesus taking care of, even while He was dying on the cross?

John 15:15. Who did Jesus no longer call servants? What did He call them instead? Why?

Was Jesus rude to us? Did He only think of what was easy and comfortable for Himself, or did He put our needs ahead of His own? He respected and showed courtesy to those around Him, in spite of their sin and their rudeness. He did this for us so He could be the perfect punishment for sin on the cross. Shouldn't we share His love with others by considering their comfort and needs?

The Bible teaches us about courtesy.

Prov. 20:11. How can we judge the character of a child? If we love Jesus, how should we treat others?

1 Sam. 16:7. What does man see when he looks at a person? Why does this make it important to show courtesy to others? What does God see? Why does this make it important to really love others in our heart?

Luke 6:43-45. What kind of fruit does a good tree produce? What kind of tree does a bad tree produce. What do our words and actions tell others about our heart?

1 Cor. 14:40. How many things should be done decently and in order? How do we do things decently?

James 3:13. What is one sign of wisdom?

Titus 3:2. How should we treat all people?

Matt. 7:12. How should we treat others? Why?

Rom. 12:10. How might you give honor to those around you?

Col. 4:6. What should your speech be like?

Additional passages to read and discuss: Phil. 2:3-4; Rom. 15:1; Luke 14:8-11; 1 Pet. 2:17

Love courteously.

- Jesus always had time for those around Him. **Read one of the gospels** and pay attention to how often He stops what He is doing to help someone or talk to someone or to bless or heal children. Notice how courteous He is to the crowds who keep following Him, those who accuse Him, those people whom others look down on, even His own disciples who don't always understand Him. Notice how He was thinking of others even while He was nailed to a cross and dying.
- **Role play different situations** to practice showing love and courtesy to others:
  - Holding a door open for someone else.
  - Saying hello to someone, even before they say hello to you.
  - Waiting to speak to someone without interrupting them.
  - Walking instead of running in church or other public places.
  - Asking someone to pass food at the table.
  - Eating politely.
  - Offering guests water, a seat, a place for their coats, etc.
  - Offering to help carry things for someone.
  - Carrying a polite conversation that focuses on the other person.
  - Being a guest in someone else's home.
  - Answering the phone courteously.
- In what ways can you treat your **parents and brothers and sisters** the way you would want to be treated? Ask God to help you see ways to be courteous all through your day.
- **Put some beans in a jar,** and set a cup next to the jar. Then see how many times you can say thank you today to those who help and bless you. Every time you say thank you, move a bean from the jar into the cup.
- **Read Matthew 25:40.** Imagine that the person you are playing or working or talking with is Jesus. How would you treat Him? That's how you should treat the person you are with, because whatever we do for others we are doing for Jesus. So treat him well!

Give thanks.

- Thank God for not despising you as a sinner, but calling you to Himself.
- Thank Him for "opening the door for you" to enter heaven and eternal life, by sending His Son to die on the cross for you.
- Thank Him for caring for you and blessing you with good things.
- Thank Jesus for becoming a man and living a life of courtesy and love so that He could die on the cross and pay the penalty for your sin.
- Thank Jesus for putting your needs ahead of His own comfort when he suffered and died for you.
- Thank Jesus for His example of courteous love.

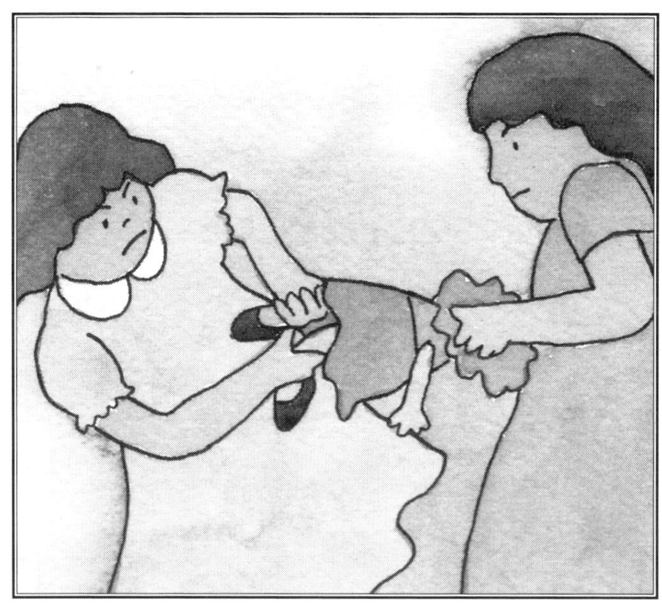

Love does not insist on its own way.

Are you thinking of others – or only about yourself?

"By this we know love, that he laid down his life for us, and we ought to lay down our lives for the brothers" (1 John 3:16).

Selfishness is concerned about its own wants and needs, but love concerns itself with the needs of others. We can't love others while we're being selfish.

Love is selfless. It seeks what is good for others. Selfishness insists on its own way.

The Greek words for *insisting on our own way* have to do with *seeking* or *striving after* our own desires. It's intense and purposeful. It is the same word that is used when King Herod was looking for baby Jesus so he could kill Him, when Jesus's parents were looking for Him on the way home from Jerusalem, and when the woman in Jesus's parable was searching for her lost coin. When we seek or insist on our own way, we don't give up easily.

- Love thinks of others. Selfishness neglects others while focusing on itself.
- Love is more concerned about doing what is good for others than it is about doing good for itself. Selfishness is more concerned about trying to do good for itself.
- Love is willing to give up its right to something for the good of someone else. Selfishness insists on its rights no matter how it affects others.
- Love is willing to give up comforts and pleasures in order to bless others. Selfishness focuses on its own comfort and pleasure.
- Love is willing to share. Selfishness keeps what is good for itself.
- Love is willing to give the best to someone else. Selfishness wants the best for itself.
- Love seeks justice for others. Selfishness only seeks justice for itself.
- Love shares in the problems of others. Selfishness overlooks the problems of others.
- Love doesn't expect anything in return. Selfishness refuses to love those who don't benefit it.
- Love remembers that the personal sacrifices it makes for others are sacrifices of love for Jesus. Selfishness doesn't want to make any sacrifices.
- Love is devoted to God and His service. Selfishness is devoted to itself.

God seeks our good.

Rom. 8:32. Who did God give up for us? What else will He give us if He gave us His Son?

1 John 4:9. How was God's love demonstrated to us? What did it accomplish?

2 Cor. 5:21. What did God do for our sake? What do we become in Christ?

Rom. 5:8. How did God show His love to us? What was our condition before Jesus died for us?

Ps. 103:2-5. What should we not forget? What has God done for us?

Additional verses to read and discuss: Matt. 7:11; John 4:10

If God was willing to give up His Son to die for us, shouldn't we, out of gratitude, be willing to make sacrifices for the sake of others?

Jesus loves selflessly.

Mark 10:45. Why did Jesus come to earth?

1 John 3:16. How do we know love? What should we do for others?

Eph. 5:2. Who is our example of love? What did He give for us?

Titus 2:14. Why did Jesus give himself for us? What did He purify us for?

2 Cor. 5:15. Who did Jesus die for? What should we do in response?

Rom. 15:3a. Did Jesus please Himself?

John 10:11. What does Jesus say He is? What does the good shepherd do?

John 10:18. Did Jesus choose to lay down His life for us? Whose will was He fulfilling?

1 Pet. 3:18. Why did Jesus, who was without sin, die for us?

2 Cor. 8:9. Why did Jesus give up His riches to become poor?

Additional verses to read and discuss: 1 Pet. 2:24; Matt. 26:39; Isa. 53:6; Eph. 1:7

Jesus willingly laid down His life for our salvation. He gave up the riches of heaven and made Himself poor in order to make us rich in Him. He suffered for our good. Now we have the privilege of sharing that love by willingly laying down our own lives and desires for the sake of others.

The Bible teaches us about selflessness.

1 Cor. 10:24. Whose good should we seek instead of our own?

Rom. 15:2-3. Who should we please? Why?

John 15:13. What is the greatest love we can have?

Rom. 12:1. Who should we give our bodies to?

Rom. 12:10. Who should we honor more than ourselves?

Phil. 2:4. Who should we be concerned about besides ourselves?

Phil. 2:5. Whose attitude should we imitate?

Rom. 14:19. What should we follow after?

Matt. 19:19. Who should we honor? Who should we love like we love ourselves?

Jer. 45:5. What should we not seek for ourselves?

Acts 20:35b. Which is better – to give or to receive?

Love selflessly.

- **Make a habit of giving the best** seat, the biggest piece, the first choice, the easiest job to someone besides yourself. Make a game of this with the family to help you become more aware of the need to do this.
- **Role play different situations** where you might be tempted to be selfish – serving dessert, playing with a special toy, sitting by the window in the car, etc. Act out the scene with a brother or sister, with both of you learning how to make the other person more important than yourself.
- Stop and ask yourself, **"How would I want to be treated"** when you are tempted to seek your own comfort and pleasure over that of someone else. (How would you want to be treated when the cake is served? That is how you should treat the other person.)
- **Get involved in a project** that helps seek the good of others who are in need of protection – unborn babies, elderly people, disabled people, single parents, etc.
- Have someone **step on your toe.** What does your body think about your toe hurting? If we are loving others, what should we think about the troubles and pain they suffer?

Give thanks.

- Thank God for giving up His only Son to suffer and die for you.
- Thank Him for taking care of you and for His promise to bless you when you bless others.
- Thank Jesus for giving up His own comfort and glory to come to earth and live a selfless life of suffering for your sake.
- Thank Jesus for seeking your good when there was nothing you could do to repay Him.
- Thank Jesus for His example of selfless love.

Love is not irritable.

Are you being cheerful – or grumpy?

"Take my yoke upon you, and learn from me, for I am gentle and lowly in heart, and you will find rest for your souls" (Matthew 11:29).

Love overlooks offenses and sins because it is seeking to meet the needs of others. Irritability finds all kinds of reason to be angry because it is concerned about its own needs. A touchy, irritable person loves himself more than he loves anyone else.

Love is peaceable. Irritability is easily angered.

The Greek word for irritability in 1 Corinthians 13:5 is translated in a number of ways – *easily provoked, easily angered, quick-tempered.* One commentator suggests the word *exasperated* as the best translation. However it is translated, it means this person is not showing love.

- A loving person knows he is loved by God and is secure and happy in that love. An irritable person expects people and circumstances to make him happy and then is disappointed by them.
- A loving person trusts God and responds calmly to life's irritating circumstances. An irritable person is irritated by every inconvenience because he isn't at peace with God,.
- Love is thankful. Irritability is ungrateful.
- Love is self-controlled. Irritability is quick-tempered.
- Love is easy-going. Irritability is easily frustrated.
- Love communicates its anger in appropriate ways. Irritability throws tantrums, cries, yells, speaks unkindly, or withdraws in anger.
- Love overlooks offenses. Irritability is easily offended.
- Love recognizes its own weaknesses and is patient with the weaknesses of others. Irritability is angered over faults and habits that are no worse than its own.
- Love uses it energy to help change anger-producing circumstances. Irritability uses its energy to quarrel and rant and hurt others.
- Love does what it can to keep peace. Irritability wants to quarrel.
- Love seeks God's help to control its anger. Irritability enjoys being angry.
- Love is free to be angry for the right reasons in a godly manner. Irritability is enslaved to anger.

God is not easily provoked.

God is not easily provoked. In fact, He is slow to anger and very patient with us. But He is rightfully angered when we turn away to worship someone or something other than Him.

Ps. 103:8. How is God described in this psalm?

Num. 14:11. What evidence did God give the Israelites that should have led them to believe Him?

Deut. 9:18. What provoked God to anger?

Deut. 31:29. What was Moses afraid the Israelites would do after he died? What did he say would provoke God to anger?

Jer. 25:6. What did God tell the people to not do? How would they provoke Him?

Ps. 78:38. How did God treat the Israelites because of His compassion? What did He not do to them? What did He restrain?

Even though we give God plenty of reasons to be angry with us, He is only provoked when we rebel and turn to other gods. If this is true, do we really have a right to be angered by those who annoy or inconvenience us? Shouldn't we give thanks for God's love and rest in it for our happiness, and then show that love to others?

Jesus's love is peaceable.

Luke 2:40. Jesus grew up in a family, and He lived a *perfect* life. Do you think He ever had any reasons to be irritated?

Mark 2:6-11. Would Jesus have good reason to be irritated with the scribes who criticized Him?

Mark 3:7-10. What are the crowds doing? Do you think Jesus ever got tired of the crowds following Him?

Mark 6:31-44. What did Jesus suggest doing with the disciples? Why? What happened? How did Jesus respond? What did Jesus do when the disciples wanted to send the people home to eat?

Mark 6:1-6. What did the people from Jesus's own hometown say about Him? How did Jesus respond?

Matt. 13:1-2. What did Jesus get into in order to speak to the people? Why do you think He did this?

Matt. 20:20-27. How did Jesus respond to the mother's request?

Matt. 26:36-45. Where were Jesus and the three disciples? What did He ask the disciples to do? What did they do instead? How did Jesus respond?

Jesus lived with brothers and sisters. He lived with parents who didn't always understand what He was doing. He was continually followed by crowds and criticized by those who envied Him. He did all this without sin – for our sakes. Does that kind of love give us the power to overlook annoyances and offenses in order to love others in the same way?

The Bible teaches us to be peaceable.

Rom. 14:19. What should we pursue?

Prov. 29:22. What does an angry man stir up? What does he cause?

Prov. 15:18. What does a hot-tempered man stir up? What does the person who is slow to anger accomplish?

Eph. 4:1-3. How do we walk in a way that is worthy of our calling?

Prov. 19:11. What does good sense or discretion lead to? What is our glory?

Prov. 17:9. How do we seek love? What ruins close friendships?

Col. 3:12-13. What are we supposed to put on, as God's children?

Prov. 14:29. What do we have when we're slow to anger? What do we exalt when we are quick-tempered?

James 1:19. What should we be quick to do? What should we be slow to be?

Prov. 20:3. What is an honor for man? Who is always quarreling?

Eccles. 7:9. What kind of person is in a hurry to get angry?

Additional verses to read and discuss: Prov. 14:17; Rom. 12:18; Heb. 12:14; Prov. 15:1

Love cheerfully.

- When you find yourself becoming irritated, **ask yourself these questions:** What is really wrong with my heart and my relationship to God that is leading to this response? How do I need to think differently about God?
- **Read one of the Gospels.** Learn about Jesus. How did He treat other people? How did He show love to others? What can you learn from His example and from His love for you?
- **Practice responding the right way** to someone or something that irritates you. The first thing you should do is pray. Ask God to help you see where your attitude is sinful. How do you need to think differently about the situation? Don't you usually need to simply overlook what is annoying you? Practice responding in a loving, godly way to people and situations that can't be overlooked.
- **Make a list** of the things that irritate you. Then **pray** about the list. **Ask** God to show you how to deal properly with these irritations.

Give thanks.

- Thank God for not punishing you, in Christ, even though your sin and rebellion deserve His anger.
- Thank Him for sending His Son to endure the trials of living among men and dying on the cross – all to save us and restore our relationship with Him.
- Thank Him for not being provoked by the many sins you still commit, and for patiently teaching you to become more like Jesus.
- Thank Jesus for loving you enough to never become angry with the irritations He faced while He lived on earth. Thank Him for living a perfect life that enabled Him to pay the punishment for your sins on the cross.
- Thank Jesus for the example of cheerful patience and forbearance that He has given us.

Love does not keep a record of wrongs.

Are you forgiving – or are you holding a grudge?

"...bearing with one another and, if one has a complaint against another, forgiving each other; as the Lord has forgiven you, so you also must forgive" (Colossians 3:13).

Love and bitterness can't coexist. Bitterness keeps a record of the wrongs it has suffered. It wants repayment. Love willingly forgives an offense because it loves without expecting anything in return.

Love is forgiving. Resentment keeps a record of wrongs.

The Greek word for *thinketh* in 1 Corinthians 13:5 means more than just *think*. It's talking about *keeping a record*. Love doesn't keep a record of *wrongs*. It doesn't have a mental ledger book where it keeps a record of all the wrongs committed against it. It's not worried about balancing the account books. It doesn't demand repayment for an offense. Instead it forgives.

- A loving person remembers that he is a sinner saved by grace. A resentful person enjoys thinking he is better than the person who wronged him.
- A loving person forgives, as he has been forgiven. A resentful person plans revenge.
- Love trusts God to judge the wrongdoer. Resentment takes over God's job.
- Love goes directly to the offender and seeks to resolve disagreements peacefully. Resentment talks to others about the offense.
- Love lets go of wrongs and starts over. A resentful person hangs onto his hurt.
- Love continues to show love when wronged. Resentment withdraws love from those who have hurt it.
- Love seeks to meet the needs of those who have hurt it. Bitterness feels no obligation to meet the needs of an offender.
- Love moves toward people without expecting anything in return. Bitterness moves away from people while demanding repayment for wrongs suffered.
- Love longs for a restored relationship. Resentment takes pleasure in hurting those who have hurt it.
- Love doesn't speak *to* the wrongdoer or *about* the wrongdoer with vengeful words. Bitterness tells others how it has been wronged.
- Love humbly repents of any sin on its part when it has been wronged. Bitterness feels noble about suffering wrongly.
- Love tries to address a wrong action. Resentment focuses on the wrongdoer.
- Love frees us from bitterness. Resentment enslaves us.
- Love makes allowances for the offenses of others and realizes that it doesn't know the whole story. Bitterness thinks it knows what the wrongdoer deserves.

God forgives us.

Neh. 9:16-17. How did God respond to the Israelites' disobedience and rebellion?

Isa. 43:25. Why does God blot out our sins?

Micah 7:18. Why does God not keep His anger forever?

1 John 1:8-9. What will God do when we confess our sins?

2 Chron. 7:14. What does God say He will do if His people humble themselves and repent?

Col. 2:13-14. How did God forgive us? What did He do with the debt we owed Him for our sin?

Ps. 130:3-4. What does God do for us? What is our response?

Ps. 103:12-14. How far has God removed our sins from us? How does God treat us? Why does He show us compassion?

Lam. 3:59. What does the writer pray for God to do?

Additional passages to read and discuss: Ps. 103:9-10; Ps. 78:38; Ps. 86:5; Rom. 5:10

When we realize that God has removed our sins from us as far as the east is from the west, we can quit keeping a record of other people's sins against us. God loves us, in Christ, and He's not holding our sins against us. Shouldn't this great love lead us to freely love and forgive others for His sake?

Jesus's love is forgiving.

Luke 7:36-50. What did the woman do for Jesus? What did Simon say about it? What did Jesus say and do?

Heb. 9:22. Whose blood earned the forgiveness of our sins?

Matt. 26:27-28. What are we remembering when we take communion? What does the wine represent?

Eph. 1:7-8. Who redeemed us from our sins?

Luke 23:34. What did Jesus say on the cross?

Luke 23:39-43. What did the two different thieves say about Jesus? What did Jesus promise the one who asked to be remembered in His kingdom?

Jesus willingly gave His life so that we could be forgiven of our sins. He paid a debt for us that we could *never* pay, and now our record is clean. We're forgiven. Shouldn't we share that same love and forgiveness with those who hurt or offend us?

The Bible teaches us about resentment.

Luke 6:36. Why should we be merciful?

Eph. 4:31-32. What should we do with bitterness? How should we forgive others? Who is our example?

Rom. 12:17-18. What should we *not* do to anyone? What should we do as much as possible?

Rom. 12:19. Why should we not avenge ourselves? What should we do instead? Who does vengeance belong to? What will He do?

Rom. 12:20-21. How should we treat our enemy? Why? How can we overcome evil?

Luke 17:3-4. What should we do if someone wrongs us? What should we do if he repents? How often should we forgive him?

Matt. 18:15-17. What four steps does Jesus outline for someone to follow when he has been wronged?

Matt. 6:14-15. How does our forgiveness of others affect how God forgives us?

Luke 6:27-28. How should we treat our enemies? Those who hate us? Those who curse us? Those who abuse us?

1 Thess. 5:15. How are we supposed to respond to evil?

1 Pet. 3:9. How should we treat those who treat us badly? Why?

Lev. 19:18. What are we supposed to do instead of getting even or bearing a grudge?

Prov. 24:17. How should we *not* respond when our enemies fall?

Additional passages to read and discuss: Matt. 18:21-25; Matt. 18:35; Col. 3:13

Love with forgiveness.

- **Read Jesus's parable in Matt. 18:23-35.** What does the story mean? Act it out with the family or with toys.
- **Read the parable of the prodigal son** again (Luke 15:11-32), paying special attention to the *father's willingness* to forgive. Did he ask the son to pay back all the money he had wasted? Did he scold him? Had the son even asked for forgiveness when the father started running to greet him? What can we learn from this story? Act it out with your family, or draw a series of pictures to illustrate it.
- **Practice asking for forgiveness.** "I was wrong for ____. I'm sorry for hurting you. Will you please forgive me?" You may need to make restitution if you have broken or lost something that belongs to the person you've wronged.
- **Practice granting forgiveness.** "Yes, I forgive you." You don't need to say anything more, unless it's "I love you". Don't scold, don't remind, don't threaten.
- When you have been wronged, **stop and ask yourself:** how would love respond to this situation? Even if you don't feel like you love the offender, do what love would do, and your love will grow.

Give thanks.

- Thank God for forgiving you, loving you, and giving you a new start in life.
- Thank Him for not keeping a record of your sin.
- Thank Him for not making you pay the punishment for your sin.
- Thank Jesus for taking the punishment for all your sins.
- Thank Him for not resenting you and all the rest of us who caused His death on the cross.

Love does not rejoice in iniquity. Love does rejoice with the truth.

Are you taking pleasure in the sins of others – or are you delighting in seeing them do well?

"...but God shows his love for us in that while we were still sinners, Christ died for us" (Romans 5:8).

It is impossible to love others well if we aren't honest about our own sin. If we don't see the need for God's saving grace in our own lives, we won't see the need to show that love and grace to other needy sinners. Instead we will tend to look down on others and use their sin to make us feel better about ourselves.

Love isn't happy about sin. It rejoices with the truth.

Two different Greek words are translated as *rejoice* in this verse. Love doesn't *celebrate* or *rejoice exceedingly* over wrongdoing. Instead it *congratulates* or *rejoices along with* truth. Love finds great joy in experiencing God's saving grace, following what is right and true, and seeing others do the same.

- A loving person is grateful for God saving him from his sins, and is eager to help others experience that same saving grace.
- Love doesn't take pleasure in seeing others sin. It prays for their repentance and faith in Jesus.
- A loving person doesn't use the sins of others as an excuse for his own sin. He is eager to live a life of obedience to God and prays that others will be, too.
- A loving person doesn't use the sins of others to make himself feel like he is good enough to please God. He is happy because faith in Jesus's death on the cross is what actually makes him and others righteous in God's sight.
- Love doesn't take pleasure in reporting on the sins of others. It is happy when it sees others obeying God and seeks to encourage them.
- Love doesn't delight in seeing sinners punished. It is eager to see sinners restored.
- Love doesn't take pleasure in speaking about the sins of others. It is eager to praise the good works of others.
- Love doesn't just see what others are doing wrong. It notices and commends what is good and praiseworthy.
- Love doesn't take pleasure in continuing to sin. It is humble and grateful when others confront it with the truth of God's Word, and eager to live a life of obedience to God.

God's love rejoices with the truth.

Deut. 32:4. How does this verse describe God? What is He without?

Ex. 34:6. What does God say He abounds in?

Ps. 33:4. How are all God's works done?

Ps. 100:5. How long will God's truth last?

Matt. 18:14. Does God *want* to punish us?

Eze. 33:11. In what does God *not* take pleasure? What does He desire?

1 Tim. 2:4-6. What does God want for all men? Who did God send as the mediator between Himself and man? What is a mediator? What did Jesus do for us?

Additional verses to read and discuss: Prov. 17:15; Jer. 9:24; Heb. 1:9

God hates sin. He longs for all to be saved and come to the knowledge of His truth, so He sent His Son to die for us. Because of God's great love, we're freed from slavery to sin, and freed to live in the truth of God's Word. Shouldn't that kind of love lead us to reach out in love to the lost and to share God's saving grace with them?

Jesus's love rejoices with the truth.

Luke 19:10. Why did Jesus come to earth?

Matt. 23:37-39. Why was Jesus grieving over Jerusalem? What did He want to do for the city? What was their response?

John 1:17. What came by Jesus?

1 John 3:5. Why did Jesus appear? Why was He qualified to do this?

John 14:6. What did Jesus say He was? How do we come to God the Father?

Isa. 61:1-3. What did God anoint Jesus to do?

Luke 4:1-13. Did Jesus choose to sin, or did He "rejoice with the truth"? How did Jesus use the truth to resist the temptations of Satan?

Read these accounts of Jesus encountering evil. How did He respond? Matt. 9:1-8; Matt. 12:1-14; Mark 1:21-28; Mark 5:1-20; Mark 9:14-29; Luke 11:37- 44; Luke 13:10-17; Luke 14:1-6; Luke 19:45-46

Jesus's life was the embodiment of God's truth. His life was devoted to proclaiming the truth and setting people free from the power of sin. This ultimately lead Him to the cross, where He conquered sin and set us free through the power of His death and resurrection. If Jesus hates sin enough to leave the glory of heaven, live as a man, and suffer and die on the cross in order to free us, shouldn't we hate sin, too, and long to see others freed from its power, through the saving grace of God?

The Bible teaches us about sin and truth.

1 John 1:6. Are we telling the truth if we say we are believers but live sinful lives?

1 John 2:4. Can we live in fellowship with God and not obey Him?

Prov. 16:6. What gets rid of sin? How do men depart from evil?

Titus 2:11-14. What brings salvation to all men? What are we to deny? How are we to live? Why did Jesus give Himself?

John 8:32. What will the truth do for us?

Rom. 12:9. What should our love be like? How should we feel about evil? What should we do with good?

3 John 1:11. What should we not imitate? What should we imitate? What is an evildoer's relationship to God?

Ps. 1:1-2. Who is blessed? What does he delight in instead of sin?

Ps. 24:17. How should we respond when our enemy falls?

Eph. 4:25. What are we supposed to put away? What should we do instead? Why?

Ps. 141:5. How should we respond when a godly person corrects us?

Additional verses to read and discuss: Isa. 1:16; Lev. 19:16; Luke 6:45; Eph. 4:29; 2 Jn. 1:4; 3 Jn. 1:3-4

Love by rejoicing with the truth.

- **Memorize 1 Corinthians 15:3-4** as a summary of the gospel, and be ready to share it with those who need Jesus.
- What **sins in your life** are keeping you from showing God's love to others? Ask your parents for help in seeing these. Repent of these sins, and pray for God's strength to overcome them. Memorize verses to arm yourself against temptation.
- **Pray for your family and friends.** Pray that their knowledge of God's amazing, unfailing love for them will increase. Pray that they will grow in their love for Jesus. Pray that they will resist the temptation to sin. Pray that unsaved friends will put their faith in Jesus, and pray for opportunities to share the gospel with them.
- **Read Matthew 18: 15-17.** Following the steps outlined in these verses, role play how to humbly confront a person who is sinning, before getting other people involved. (Doorposts' *Brother-Offended Chart* teaches this in detail.)
- **Read the parable in Luke 18:9-14.** Was the Pharisee sharing God's love with sinners and rejoicing in the truth of God's grace for sinners, or was he happy to use their sins as a way to make him feel spiritually better than they were?

Give thanks.

- Thank God for forgiving you and providing a way, even though He hates sin, for you to be saved from sin and its punishment and restored to fellowship with Him.
- Thank God for giving us His Word, which is the source of all truth about God and life.
- Thank Him for giving you the Holy Spirit who is teaching you God's truth and helping you to overcome sin.
- Thank Jesus for bringing the truth of God's love to the world.
- Thank Him for hating sin and loving you enough to die in your place.
- Thank Jesus for defeating sin and death and freeing you to live a life of obedience to God.

Love bears all things.

Are you quietly persevering – or are you complaining?

"He was oppressed, and he was afflicted, yet he opened not his mouth" (Isaiah 53:7a).

When we love ourselves in a distorted way, we tend to think we should never suffer or be wronged by others. When we understand how much God gave because of His love for us, we'll be better able to love others, quietly accepting the hardships that He allows in our lives, and reaching out to help bear the burdens of others.

Love is forbearing.

The Greek word for *bears* in this verse has to do with *covering* and especially *covering over with silence.* A loving person bears his own trials quietly, while also quietly covering the sins of others rather than publicizing them. The word also speaks of *supporting* something, as walls that support a roof. Love bears all annoyances, troubles, and wrongs without complaining.

- Love quietly continues to love, even when people or circumstances are difficult.
- Love continues loving even when it has been wronged, and does so without telling everyone else about it.
- Love reproves someone of sin privately, but does not publicize the sin.
- Love covers over the faults and mistakes of others whenever it can rightfully do so.
- Love doesn't take pleasure in discovering or exposing the sins of others.
- Love seeks the wisdom of God to discern when it is best to expose the sins of others, and when it is best to keep their sin confidential, allowing time for repentance and healing to happen behind the scenes.
- Love seeks to protect the sinner from the gossip and sinful judgment of others.
- Love comes alongside those who are suffering and helps carry their burdens.
- Love is willing to ignore as much as possible the sins of unbelievers in order to share God's love and the gospel with them.
- Love continues to share the love of God with unbelievers, even when it is rejected or mocked.

God bears with us.

Ps. 103:13-14. How does God treat us? What does he remember about us?

Rom. 2:4. Why is God kind to us?

Isa. 53:6. What did God do for us when we went astray?

Ps. 78:38-39. What did God do because of His compassion? What does He remember about man?

God shows great patience and kindness to us as He leads us to repentance. He remembers how weak we are. While we were still sinners, He reached out to us, and laid the burden of our sin onto Jesus, who suffered and died for us. Shouldn't we show patience and kindness to those who, like us, are weak, and shouldn't we reach out to show God's love and patience to those who are still lost and need Jesus?

Jesus bears our sins.

John 1:11. When Jesus came to His people, how did they treat Him? Did Jesus quit loving them because of this?

1 Pet. 2:23-24. How did Jesus respond when He was mocked? What did He not do when He was threatened? Who did He commit Himself to? Why did He do this?

Isa. 53:4-7. What did Jesus bear for us? How did we treat Him? Why did He do this? What did His suffering accomplish for us? What did Jesus not do when He was mistreated and beaten? What is He compared to?

Matt. 8:17. What did Jesus take onto Himself? What did He bear for us?

Matt. 27:12-14. How did Jesus respond when He was accused by the chief priests and elders? How did He respond to Pilate's question?

John 19:17. What did Jesus bear?

Matt. 26:53. What could Jesus have done if He had chosen to?

Matt. 11:28-29. What will Jesus give to us when we come to Him?

Heb. 4:15. Why does Jesus have compassion for us in our sin?

Rom. 8:34. Who makes intercession or pleads for us at God's right hand in heaven? Why is He qualified to do this?

Read and discuss these accounts of Jesus's love for sinners that others looked down on: Matt. 9:9-12; Mark 14:3-9; Luke 15:1-7; Luke 19:1-10.

Jesus, because He loved us so much, was willing to suffer for us – without complaint. He endured the insults and mockery of the very ones He came to save, and bore the punishment for all our sins on the cross. Shouldn't we be able to bear quietly with the wrongdoings of other sinners like ourselves? Shouldn't we, with the enabling of the Holy Spirit, be willing to bear with the sins and insults of the unsaved in order to give them the good news of Christ's saving death and resurrection?

The Bible teaches us about forbearance.

Rom. 15:1. What do we have a duty to do? Who should we not worry about pleasing?

Prov. 10:12. What does hatred stir up? What does love cover?

1 Pet. 4:8. What is the most important thing we should have toward each other? Why?

Eph. 4:2. How do we treat each other in love?

Col. 3:13. How should we treat each other? What should we do if we have a disagreement with someone? Who is our example?

Prov. 17:9. What are we seeking when we choose to cover someone's sin? What happens when we choose to broadcast those sins?

Gal. 6:1-2. How should we treat a believer who is sinning? What should our attitude be? How do we fulfill the law of Christ?

Love quietly.

- **Read John 4:6-30.** Talk about this story. Why was the woman surprised that Jesus would talk to her? Why were the disciples surprised? Would Jesus have been able to serve the woman and help her if He had been unwilling to sit down and talk with her? What can we learn from His example as we seek to share the gospel with the unsaved?
- **Read the story of the Good Samaritan in Luke 10:30-37.** Then act it out. Why do you think the priest and the Levite pass by on the other side of the road? What was the Samaritan willing to do for the man? What did the Jews think of Samaritans?
- **Role play** different situations where you would be tempted to complain or report the wrongdoings of others when it would have been better to cover those wrongs with love. Also practice using the right words to correct someone for their sin, when that proves necessary.
    - Someone says something unkind to you.
    - Your brother takes a toy from you.
    - Someone makes fun of you.
    - A sister takes the bigger piece of dessert.
- **Find a way to serve the unsaved with your family.** Can you serve food at a rescue mission; take blankets to the homeless; invite people into your home for meals; talk to unsaved people who don't "fit in" at church?

Give thanks.

- Thank God for His patience and forbearance with your sins as He brought you to repentance and salvation.
- Thank Him for sending His Son to live among sinful, wicked men in order to die for us and save us.
- Thank God for His continued patience and forbearance as He works to make us more like Jesus.
- Thank Jesus for His willingness to become a man and live among us, living a perfect life and bearing the punishment for our sins.
- Thank Him for helping you to bear your troubles and challenges in life.

Love believes all things.

Are you trusting people – and God – or are you doubting their word?

"...when he suffered, he did not threaten, but continued entrusting himself to him who judges justly"
(1 Peter 2:23b).

When we love, we are willing to entrust ourselves to God so that we can love people, even if it sometimes means being hurt or cheated. We can't love others while we are worried about them deceiving us or making fools of us. To share God's love with others, we first have to trust God's love for *us*. If we really believe God loves us and only allows what is ultimately good in our lives, we'll trust Him and we'll be ready to love others without holding back.

Love is willing to trust.

The Greek word for *believes* in 1 Corinthians 13:7 means *to be persuaded of* or *to place confidence in*. As we seek to love others as God loves us, we must let down our guard and be willing to be vulnerable for the sake of others. To do this, we need to put our full confidence in God, who is always faithful. We can trust Him to work out all circumstances in our lives for our good and His glory.

- Love trusts God, which leads it to trust fellow believers, in spite of their faults.
- Love does not assume the worst, but believes the best about others for as long as it can, until forced by clear evidence to believe otherwise.
- Love gives a fallen believer grace, allowing for his weaknesses and mistakes.
- Love is quick to see the best qualities in someone, and slow to find fault.
- Love will not listen to gossip and rumors.
- Love will speak good of others.
- Love refuses to harm the reputation of others by speaking evil of them.
- Love trusts God, so it is willing to love wholeheartedly, without over-concern for being imposed upon, cheated, or hurt.
- Love is willing to risk trusting others too much and being occasionally taken advantage of, rather than trusting them too little.
- Love believes that every person is valuable and that everyone can, by God's saving grace, become good.
- A loving person believes God loves him, and is eager to share that love with others.
- Love doesn't suspect or try to outguess the secret motives of others.

- Love remembers that only God knows man's heart, and only He has the right to judge his intentions.
- Love recognizes that it is responsible for its own motives and actions, and not for those of others.
- Love continues believing in God and in what He can do in the lives of others, even in the midst of suffering and hardship.
- Love shares the gospel, because it believes that those without Christ are lost and that Christ's death and resurrection have the power to save and change them.

God is trustworthy.

2 Sam. 22:3. To what is God compared?

Job 13:15. What did Job say about God, even while he was suffering?

Job 19:25. What did Job believe about God? Do you think this made it easier to trust Him while he was suffering?

Prov. 30:5. How many of God's words are pure? For those who trust Him, what is God?

Matt. 5:45. For whom does God make the sun rise? On whom does He send rain? Does He show grace to all men?

Ps. 62:8. When should we trust God? What is God for us?

Additional passages to read and discuss: Ps. 118:8-9; 1 Pet. 4:19; Ps. 9:10; Ps. 37:3; 2 Tim. 1:12

God is completely trustworthy. He always keeps His Word. He always takes care of us. He has chosen to show us His grace, even when we were not worthy of His favor. Shouldn't we show this same kind of grace to others? Shouldn't we trust Him enough to love others without judging them and without worrying about them deceiving or taking advantage of us?

Jesus's love trusts.

Phil. 2:6-11. Was Jesus equal with God? What was He willing to do, even though He knew what it would cost Him? Who do you think He was trusting? What can we learn from His example? What did God do in response to Jesus's obedience and humility?

Mark 14:36. What did Jesus believe about God? Do you think this led Him to trust Him?

John 6:40. What did Jesus say the Father's will was? What will those who believe on Jesus receive? What will Jesus do for them?

1 Pet. 2:23. What did Jesus do when He was insulted and threatened? Who did He commit Himself to?

John 11:25. What did Jesus say He was? What will happen to those who believe in Him?

Matt. 27:46. What did Jesus cry out as He suffered on the cross? Why?

Luke 23:46. When He had finished taking our punishment, what did He say? Did Jesus trust His Father? Did He believe He had accomplished the mission God had given to Him?

Jesus was willing to love us fully, even though He knew all man's thoughts and even though He knew what we would do to Him. He loves the Father and He loves us, and He believed that God would grant forgiveness to us through His death on the cross. His love and His trust in the Father drove Him to lay down His life for us. Shouldn't that kind of love lead us to trust God and love others without worrying about what might happen to us while we love?

The Bible teaches us about trusting others.

Prov. 18:13. What is it when we come to conclusions before we have all the facts?

1 Pet. 2:1-3. What should we lay aside? What should we desire? Why?

Prov. 14:15. What kind of person believes *everything* he hears? Who looks well to his ways? What do we need in order to know when to believe others?

Ps. 112:5-7. How does a good man treat others? What is he not afraid of? Why? Who is he trusting?

Ps. 118:8-9. Who, instead of men and leaders, is better to put our trust in?

Jer. 9:4. Why do we need to have wisdom from God and ultimately put our trust in Him when dealing with others?

1 Pet. 4:19. What should we do when we suffer for doing good?

Love confidently.

- **Memorize verses about God's faithfulness** to those who trust Him, and recite them to yourself when you are tempted to not trust those around you. (Examples: Ps. 5:11; Ps. 22:4-5; Ps. 32:10; Ps. 40:4; Prov. 29:25)
- **Think about the past.** How many times have you misjudged others, or assumed the worst about them, only to find out later that you were mistaken? Have you ever ended up being good friends with someone you didn't like to start with?
- Discuss how you should respond when someone gives you a bad report about someone. Should you believe them? Should you assume the best about the person being spoken of until you see clear evidence to the contrary? What should you say to the person gossiping? **Role play this situation.**
- Reach out to someone you would not normally befriend. **Find practical ways to show God's love** to that person.
- **Copy and illustrate one of these verses about gossip and post it in your room:** Ps. 34:13; Prov. 11:9; Prov. 16:28; Eph. 4:29; Eph. 4:31; 1 Pet. 3:10.
- **What worries and concerns do you need to commit into God's hands** as you seek to love others as God loves them? Are you worried about what other people might think? Are you concerned about being taken advantage of? Are you afraid you may get hurt? Pray about these, and trust God.

Give thanks.

- Thank God for His absolute faithfulness that you can fully trust as you reach out in love to others.
- Thank Him for seeing what you can become, by His grace, and helping you grow.
- Thank Him for knowing all and for judging righteously.
- Thank Jesus for His example of loving trust in His Father and self-sacrificing love for you.
- Thank Jesus for loving you when you were still unsaved, and for believing in God's power to change you.

Love hopes all things.

Are you believing – or forgetting – God's promises?

"...looking to Jesus, the founder and perfecter of our faith, who for the joy that was set before him endured the cross, despising the shame, and is seated at the right hand of the throne of God" (Hebrews 12:2).

Love and hope feed each other. Without love, we give up hope for those who seem hopeless. When we give in to despair and quit hoping, our love begins to fade. Because we are loved by God, we can continue loving and hoping for God's changing work in the lives of those we love.

Love believes God's promises.

Biblical hope is not wishful thinking. It is *certainty.* It is a confident, joyful expectation of good – and more specifically, of eternal salvation -- based on the character, word, and actions of God. We *know* that righteousness will ultimately be victorious, and Christ's resurrection is the guarantee of that victory. Because Jesus has already won the victory, we can continue hoping for His transforming work in the lives of others, even when everything appears hopeless.

- Love continues to hope and pray for the restoration and repentance of a sinner, when others have given up, because it does not give up on what God can do.
- A loving person continues to hope in all situations, because he has experienced the steadfast love of God and knows that God wants what is best for us.
- A loving person continues to hope in all situations because he believes the promise of God's final victory, even if problems are not solved in his present life.
- A loving person looks beyond immediate solutions to life's problems and hardships, and rests his hope in the sure promises of God – promises that assure us that He is glorified and that we are refined as we live with difficult people and circumstances.
- A loving person continues to love and pray for those who appear to be hopeless in their sin and rebellion, because he knows that God's love has the power to make all things new.
- A loving person believes that love and hope will ultimately win over sin and indifference, and that all wrongs will be made right.
- Love places its hope in Christ, who will not – and cannot – fail, because He has already won the victory.
- Love knows that because of Jesus's death and resurrection, there is always hope, no matter how hopeless the person or situation may look.

God gives us hope.

Heb. 10:23. Why can we hold fast in our faith?

2 Tim. 4:7-8. What is God going to give us when we He returns?

Titus 1:2. What did God promise us before the world began? Does God keep His Word?

Eph. 1:18-21. What will we understand when God opens our eyes? How did God give us hope and an inheritance with other believers? Who did He exalt?

1 Pet. 1:3-5. How has God the Father given us hope? What is waiting for us in heaven? Who is taking care of us until we receive our inheritance?

1 Pet. 1:6-9. What may we still experience, even while we rejoice over what God has in store for us? What is God accomplishing in our lives through trials? Whom do we love, even though we can't see Him? What is the result of believing what God has promised?

Jer. 29:11. What are the thoughts God has toward us?

Rom. 15:13. Who fills us with joy and hope as we trust Him? Who causes us to overflow with hope?

Luke 1:37. What is impossible for God to do?

Ps. 130:7. Why should we hope in the Lord?

God is the reason for our hope. We know what God can do. We've experienced His love and life-changing power in our lives, and He promises that one day we will be like Jesus and all the wrongs of the world will be made right. Shouldn't we keep expecting God to do great things in the lives of others? Shouldn't we continue showing His love to others, even if we receive nothing in return?

Jesus loved expectantly.

Rom. 5:6-8. What did we not have when Christ died for us? Are most people willing to die for someone else – even for someone who is good? How did God show His love to us? What were we like when Jesus died for us?

Titus 2:13. What is our hope?

1 John 3:2. What will we be like when we see Jesus?

1 Cor. 15:19-22. Is Jesus only our hope in this life on earth? If we all died when Adam sinned, what do we all gain because Jesus rose from the dead? How does this give us hope?

Read and discuss the following accounts of Jesus meeting and talking to the following people. How did He demonstrate hope for each of these people? Nicodemus, John 3:1-21; Zacchaeus, Luke 19:1-10; the dying thief, Luke 23:39-43; the rich young man, Matt. 19:16-22; Saul, Acts 9:1-19; woman taken in adultery, John 8:3-11; the disciples, Luke 22:24-27; Peter, Luke 22:31-34, 54-62

Jesus knew His Father loved Him, and that He would accomplish all that He promised to accomplish through Christ's death on the cross. So Jesus lived a life of hope, always looking at people and seeing what they could become, by the saving power of God. That hope ultimately led Him to the cross, where He died, knowing God would raise Him from the dead, and that His death and resurrection would win eternal life for those who believed in Him.

If Jesus gave up His life to give us new life, shouldn't we hope for that same new life for others? If He is willing to forgive us, shouldn't we remember that He is just as willing to forgive those that we think are beyond forgiveness? Shouldn't we lay down our lives in love for the hopeless, knowing that ultimately God will reward our hope?

The Bible teaches us about hope.

Rom. 5:1-5. Who enabled us to have peace with God? In what do we rejoice? What do trials produce? What does patience give us? What gives us hope? And what does hope do?

Ps. 31:24. What should we have when we hope in the Lord? What will God do for us?

Prov. 10:28. What does our hope bring? What happens to the hope of the wicked?

Ps. 119:81. What do we hope in?

Rom. 12:12. What should we rejoice in? What should we be patient in? What should we continue in?

1 Thess. 5:8-11. What should we put on as a breastplate? What should we wear as a helmet? What has God appointed for us to receive? Who do we live with, both when we are alive and when we die?

Love expectantly.

- Is there someone in your life that you are tired of trying to love? Have you lost hope for them? **Pray** again for that person. Pray for yourself and for a renewal of hope and love. **Reach out** to the person and show him love, not expecting anything in return, but remembering that God can do the impossible.
- **Read Heb. 11:1-31.** Stop to talk about each person listed in this passage. Use a concordance to find and read the account of each person's life. How did each person demonstrate his or her hope in God? **Act out** each of these stories, or make a book that illustrates each person's life of hope and faith.
- **Interview your parents, grandparents, or other adults believers.** How has God proven Himself faithful in their lives? Have they ever had times when they were tempted to give up hope? What did they do? What did God do?

Give thanks.

- Thank God for never giving up on you.
- Thank Him for saving you and continuing to work in your life to make you more like His Son.
- Thank Him for giving His Son to die for our sins, and for the power He has to change the lives of those you are tempted to view as hopeless.
- Thank Him for the grace He gives you to continue loving those you are tempted to give up on.
- Thank Jesus for dying for you when you were hopeless in your own sin.
- Thank Him for giving you the hope of resurrection and eternal life.

Love endures all things.

Are you standing fast – or are you giving up?

"And being found in human form, he humbled himself by becoming obedient to the point of death, even death on a cross" (Philippians 2:8).

Love keeps on loving no matter what. If we're giving up, we can be sure that we're giving up on loving, too.

Love perseveres to the end.

The Greek word for *endure* is made up of two smaller words. One means *to remain* and the other means *under* or *by*. It is a military term that speaks of standing fast in the thick of battle without retreating. When we endure, we stand firm under trials and persecutions instead of running from them. We remain *by* those who persecute or wrong us, because they still need God's love.

- Love responds to unkindness with kindness.
- Love keeps on loving, even while facing the assaults of sinful people.
- Love actively endures affliction and trials without complaint or resentment.
- Love accepts trials with patience, and endures them with courage and faith.
- Love does not give in to evil, but perseveres, seeking to overcome evil with good.
- Love does not back down. It keeps bravely and calmly loving and forgiving in spite of ill treatment or persecution, and does not give in to unkindness, anger, or resentment.
- Love keeps loving and praying, even when someone continues to grow worse instead of better.
- Love suffers with and for others because it becomes actively involved in the lives of others.
- Love endures with joy, no matter how it is treated, because it knows that it is sharing in the sufferings of Christ.
- Love continues to share God's love, even when it is mocked or rejected.
- Love perseveres in loving its enemies with courage and strength.
- Love endures, looking forward with hope to God's promised reward for those who persevere.
- A loving person grows in his faith and strength as he endures whatever God brings into His life.

God rewards endurance.

Col. 1:20-23. What did God accomplish through Christ's blood? How did God reconcile all things to Himself? What did God do for us while we were His enemies? What will God do for us if we persevere in the faith?

Rev. 3:21. What does Jesus promise to those who endure?

Matt. 10:22. How will men treat us for Jesus's sake? What does Jesus promise to those who endure?

Rom. 2:6-7. What does God give to those who patiently continue doing good?

James 1:12. What has God promised to those who love Him and remain steadfast under trials?

Heb. 10:35-39. Why should we not throw away our confidence in God? Why do we need to endure?

Col. 1:11. Who gives us the strength to endure?

Rom. 8:38-39. What can separate us from God's love?

God doesn't ask us to stand fast in our own strength when we suffer trials. He loves us and stands beside us, giving us strength and courage, and reminding us of the eternal life and crown that awaits us. Do we really have any reason to give up when God so faithfully loves and upholds us?

Jesus loves to the end.

Heb. 12:1-4. What should we set aside? How should we run? Who should we look to for our example? What motivated Jesus to endure the cross? Have we suffered as much as Jesus did?

John 13:1. How did Jesus treat those He loved, even as His crucifixion drew near?

Gal. 2:20. Who are we crucified with? Who lives in us? How do we live our lives? What did Jesus do for us?

Rom. 8:35-37. What can separate us from the love of Christ? Who gives us the victory? Who does He love?

Luke 22:44. Was Jesus suffering, even before He was arrested and crucified?

Isa. 50:6. What did Jesus suffer? Did He hide from persecution?

Mark 15:34. What did God the Father do while Jesus was bearing our sins on the cross? Did Jesus give up?

John 15:13 tells us, "Greater love has no one than this, that someone lays down his life for his friends." **Read the account of Christ's crucifixion** in Matt. 27:28-50 and notice all that Jesus endured as He laid down His life for us. Thank Him for His great love for you.

Because of His great love for us and for His Father, Jesus endured suffering to the point of tortuous death on a cross. The same God who gave Jesus the strength to endure will also strengthen us in our trials. The same loving God who raised Jesus from the dead and exalted Him above all names will also give us eternal life and the privilege of reigning with Jesus. If we really believe that God loves us and that He keeps His promises, why would we ever consider giving up in the midst of trials?

The Bible teaches us about endurance.

2 Cor. 12:9-10. Where is God's strength made perfect? Why can we glory in our weaknesses? For whose sake can we take joy in suffering persecution and trials? What are we, in Christ, when we are weak?

2 Cor. 4:17-18. How long do our trials last on earth? What do they accomplish? What should we look at? Why?

1 Pet. 1:6-7. What is the trial of our faith more precious than? When will it be praised and honored?

Heb. 11:24-27. What did Moses give up in order to suffer affliction with the Israelites? What did he consider better than the riches of Egypt? Why?

Matt. 16:24-25. What does following Jesus require? What happens to the person who tries to save his life? What happens to the one who is willing to lose his life?

Matt. 5:10-12. What belongs to those who are persecuted for righteousness' sake? What does Jesus say we are when men persecute us for His sake? Why should we rejoice when we are persecuted for Jesus's sake? Who else was persecuted?

2 Tim. 2:1-12. What should we be strong in? What should we endure? What are we to be like? If we suffer with Jesus, what else will we do with Him?

1 Pet. 5:8-10. What is the devil like? What should we remember while we are resisting the devil and standing firm in our faith? What will God do after we have suffered for a while?

Additional passages to read and discuss: Matt. 5:44-45; Lk. 6:27-36; Rom. 12:14; 1 Cor. 16:13

Love with endurance.

- **Read Heb. 11:32-40.** Discuss the many ways believers throughout history have endured in faith. Would you be willing to suffer in these ways? Would God give you the strength and grace to endure, if He called you to? Illustrate these verses in some way – with drawings, Lego or Playmobil set ups, dramas with your siblings, or some other method.
- **Are there people in your life you would count as enemies?** Pray about your relationship with those people. Ask God to help you see ways that you have contributed to the problem. Repent of any sinful attitudes and actions – both to God and to the people involved. Start praying for your enemies. Pray for God's healing in their lives. Ask God to bless them, and to show them His love through you.
- **Read one of the Gospels** and pay special attention to Jesus as He endures the hatred and abuse of His enemies. What can you learn from His example? Where did He get His strength to continue loving those who did not love Him?
- **Read *The Hiding Place*** or watch the movie version of the story. Talk about the main characters' responses to evil and mistreatment and the grace God gave them to love their enemies. What can you learn and apply in your relationships?

Give thanks.

- Thank God for loving you when you didn't love Him, and for drawing you to Him.
- Thank God for the gift of eternal life that He gives to those who faithfully endure.
- Thank Him for the strength and grace He gives you to keep on loving while you endure difficult people and circumstances.
- Thank Jesus for enduring the suffering of the cross because of His faithful love for you.
- Thank Him for His example of loving people where they were and seeing what they could become by God's grace and power.
- Thank Him for loving you and showing you how to love.